Land of Liberty

South Carolina

by Sandra J. Christian,
M.Ed

Consultant:
Paul A. Horne Jr.
Executive Director
South Carolina Council
for the Social Studies

Capstone
press
Mankato, Minnesota

Capstone Press
151 Good Counsel Drive • P.O. Box 669 • Mankato, Minnesota 56002
http://www.capstone-press.com

Library of Congress Cataloging-in-Publication Data
Christian, Sandra J.
    South Carolina / by Sandra J. Christian.
    p. cm.—(Land of liberty)
    Includes bibliographical references and index.
    Contents: About South Carolina—Land, climate, and wildlife—History of
South Carolina—Government and politics—Economy and resources—People and
culture—Recipe: Gullah rice pudding—South Carolina's flag and seal.
    ISBN 0-7368-2197-X (hardcover)
    1. South Carolina—Juvenile literature. [1. South Carolina.] I. Title. II. Series.
F269.3.C49 2004
975.7—dc21   2003001293

Summary: An introduction to the geography, history, government, politics,
    economy, resources, people, and culture of South Carolina, including maps,
    charts, and a recipe.

Editorial Credits

Megan Schoeneberger, editor; Jennifer Schonborn, series designer; Linda Clavel,
book designer; Enoch Peterson, illustrator; Alta Schaffer, photo researcher; Eric
Kudalis, product planning editor

Photo Credits

Cover images: South Carolina plantation, PhotoDisc Inc.; Myrtle Beach, Folio
Inc./Dennis Johnson

Augusta Chronicle, 50; Capstone Press/Gary Sundermeyer, 54; Corbis, 33, 56, 63;
Corbis/Bettman, 36; Corbis/Bob Krist, 48; Corbis/Historical Picture Archive, 20;
Corbis/Richard Bickel, 4; Corbis/Will & Deni McIntyre, 42; Creatas, 19; Folio
Inc./David R. Frazier, 40; Folio Inc./Dennis Johnson, 46–47; Getty Images/
Hulton Archive, 23, 24, 26, 29, 31, 58; Houserstock/Dave G. Houser, 8; One
Mile Up Inc., 55 (both); PhotoDisc Inc., 1; Transparencies Inc./James H. Reeves,
12–13; Transparencies Inc./Jane Faircloth, 16–17, 34, 45, 52–53; Transparencies
Inc./Kelly Culpepper, 18; Transparencies Inc./Michael Moore, 14; U.S. Postal
Service, 59; Visuals Unlimited/Glenn M. Oliver, 57

Artistic Effects

Corbis, Linda Clavel, PhotoDisc Inc.

1 2 3 4 5 6 08 07 06 05 04 03

Table of Contents

Waves wash across the shore of Pawleys Island, where people often report seeing the ghost of the Gray Man before hurricanes.

Chapter 1

About South Carolina

Off South Carolina's coast, winds begin to swirl. The ocean churns, and waves crash against each other. Heavy clouds hang in the dark sky. Rain pours down. Slowly, the hurricane moves closer to land.

On the shore of Pawleys Island, some people think they see a ghostly gray figure. It warns people to find safety. Most likely, the figure is a trick of light and shadow, fooling the eye. But many people swear they have seen the ghost of the Gray Man.

Since 1893, people have reported seeing the ghost before every major hurricane. Oddly, the people who follow his warnings are usually spared from the storm's heavy rains, flooding, and strong winds.

The Palmetto State

South Carolina's nickname is "The Palmetto State." Palmetto palm trees are a symbol of strength in South Carolina. Palmettos grow along the Atlantic coast of the state. During the Revolutionary War (1775–1783), troops led by Colonel William Moultrie used palmettos to build Fort Moultrie on Sullivan's Island in Charleston Harbor. In an important battle, American colonists defeated British soldiers at the fort.

South Carolina is small and shaped like a triangle. It covers 32,007 square miles (82,898 square kilometers), making it the 11th smallest state. More than 4 million people live in the state. The Atlantic Ocean lies on the state's eastern border. North Carolina lies to the north. To the south and west is Georgia.

South Carolina's Cities

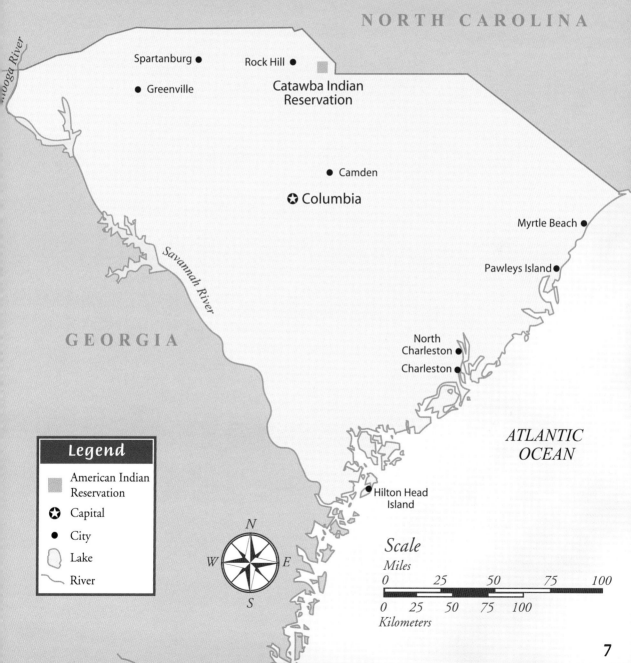

NORTH CAROLINA

Spartanburg •

Rock Hill •

Catawba Indian
Reservation

• Greenville

• Camden

✪ Columbia

Myrtle Beach •

Pawleys Island •

GEORGIA

North
Charleston •

Charleston •

ATLANTIC
OCEAN

• Hilton Head
Island

Savannah River

...ooga River

Legend

■	American Indian Reservation
✪	Capital
•	City
⬭	Lake
〰	River

N
W E
S

Scale

Miles

0   25   50   75   100

0   25   50   75   100

Kilometers

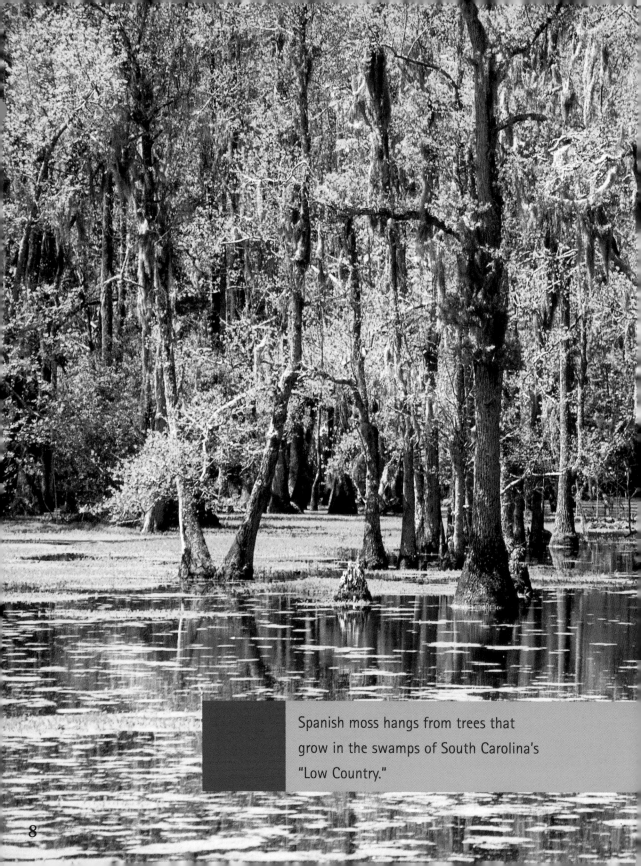

Spanish moss hangs from trees that grow in the swamps of South Carolina's "Low Country."

Chapter 2

Land, Climate, and Wildlife

Often, the people of South Carolina divide their state into two main regions. They call the land closest to the Atlantic Ocean the "Low Country." The rest of the state makes up what South Carolinians call the "Up Country."

South Carolina's landscape stretches from the blue ocean to the Blue Ridge Mountains. The Coastal Zone borders the Atlantic Ocean. From there, the land slowly slopes across the Coastal Plain to the Sandhills. Beyond the Sandhills, the land rises suddenly to the Piedmont Plateau. The Blue Ridge Mountains, part of the Appalachian Mountains, lie in South Carolina's northwestern corner.

The Coastal Zone and Coastal Plain

The Coastal Zone borders the Atlantic Ocean. Measured in a straight line, South Carolina has 187 miles (301 kilometers) of sandy coastline. Counting the coastlines of all of South Carolina's bays, inlets, and islands, the coastline becomes longer than the Mississippi River.

Small, swampy islands off the state's shores also are part of the Coastal Zone. These islands are called barrier islands. They block the mainland from the ocean's large waves and heavy winds.

The largest region in South Carolina is the Coastal Plain. Two smaller parts make up the Coastal Plain. The flat, sandy Outer Coastal Plain lies closest to the Atlantic Ocean. Farther inland, the Inner Coastal Plain is hilly. Farmers use this land to grow cotton and soybeans.

The Sandhills and the Piedmont Plateau

The Sandhills region stretches across the middle of South Carolina. The land is hilly and sandy. Long ago, the Atlantic Ocean reached to the Sandhills. Over time, the level of ocean water became lower. As more land became dry, the coastline moved to where it is today.

South Carolina's Land Features

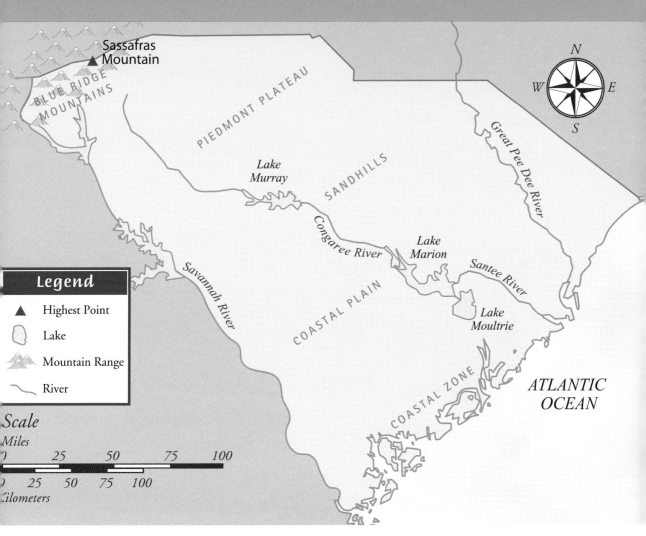

Next to the Sandhills is the Piedmont Plateau. Piedmont means "at the foot of the mountains." The rocky region reaches to the Blue Ridge Mountains. Small, single mountains called monadnocks rise above the rocky land. Paris Mountain, Kings Mountain, and Table Rock Mountain are monadnocks.

Between the Sandhills and the Piedmont Plateau, the land rises sharply. The sudden rise creates a drop-off called the fall line. Above the fall line, rivers flow fast. Below the fall line, rivers flow more slowly. Rapids and waterfalls form where rivers flow over the drop-off.

The Blue Ridge Mountains

The Piedmont meets the Blue Ridge Mountains in the northwestern corner of South Carolina. These mountains are

older than the Rocky Mountains and other mountains in the West. Over time, wind and water have worn them down. They are shorter than many other mountains. Sassafras Mountain, the state's highest point, reaches 3,560 feet (1,085 meters) above sea level in this region. Raven Cliff Falls is also in this region. At 420 feet (128 meters), it is South Carolina's tallest waterfall.

Rivers and Lakes

South Carolina's rivers flow from west to east toward the Atlantic Ocean. The Santee River is 143 miles (230 kilometers) long. It is the longest river that flows entirely within the state.

Forests around Table Rock Mountain in northwestern South Carolina fill with color in fall. The Cherokee Indians believed the Great Spirit used the mountain for a dinner table.

Other major rivers include the Great Pee Dee, the Congaree, and the Savannah Rivers.

The largest lakes in South Carolina have not been there for long. In 1930, engineers built the Saluda Dam to provide

People use Lake Murray and other lakes in South Carolina for recreation.

electricity to the area around
Columbia. Before building the
dam, they moved 5,000 people,
three churches, six schools, and
2,000 graves. Water pooled up
behind the dam to form Lake
Murray. This large lake covers
50,000 acres (20,235 hectares).
In the early 1940s, water behind the Santee Dam on the
Santee River formed Lake Marion and Lake Moultrie.

Climate

South Carolina's climate is warm and wet. Warm ocean
breezes bring humidity to the state. Most of the state receives
about 48 inches (122 centimeters) of precipitation each year.
Nearly all of this amount falls as rain in spring and summer.

South Carolina's winters are short and mild. The Blue
Ridge Mountains block cold air from the north. Each winter
has short cold spells, but they rarely last very long. Snow
sometimes falls in the mountains and upper Piedmont
Plateau. Snow rarely falls in the rest of the state.

South Carolina's long, hot summers give the state a long growing season. Farmers near the coast can plant crops at the end of February without danger of a killing frost. They can grow plants until early December. Mountain areas often have about six months to grow crops before a frost hits.

Plant Life

South Carolina's climate is perfect for wildflowers and flowering shrubs. Yellow jessamines, flowering dogwoods, and azaleas grow throughout the state.

Besides palmettos, South Carolina has many trees. Forests cover two-thirds of the state. Pine, magnolia, and hemlock trees are common in the state. Cypress trees and live oak trees grow in swampy areas. Spanish moss often hangs from their wide branches.

Wildlife

South Carolina has more types of birds than most other states. Ducks, geese, and gulls follow the same migration route along South Carolina's coast each year. Pelicans build nests along

Colorful azalea blossoms line the streets of Summerville in March and April.

Angel Oak

The Angel Oak has stood through wars and hurricanes. More than 1,000 years ago, an acorn dropped into the ground near what is now Charleston. From this tiny acorn grew one of the largest live oak trees in the world.

The Angel Oak is very wide. It provides more than 17,000 square feet (1,580 square meters) of shade. To circle the thick trunk, about seven people would need to stand around it holding hands.

the coast. Wild turkeys, mourning doves, and bald eagles live throughout South Carolina. Songbirds include cardinals, blue jays, swallows, and the Carolina wren.

Barrier islands and swampy lowlands are home to reptiles and amphibians. South Carolina has lizards, turtles, and more than 40 types of snakes. Copperheads, water moccasins, coral snakes, and rattlesnakes are venomous snakes found in South Carolina. Alligators can be found as far inland as Columbia. Salamanders, frogs, toads, and other amphibians are common.

Most mammals in South Carolina are small. Raccoons, otters, and skunks are native animals. The most common animals are foxes, squirrels, and rabbits. Some black bears and bobcats roam forests and swampy areas far from cities.

South Carolina's wet, swampy lowlands contain many alligators. The longest alligator ever found in the state was about 13 feet (4 meters) long.

Some American Indians in South Carolina used bows and arrows to hunt.

Chapter 3

History of South Carolina

When Europeans first came to present-day South Carolina, they met American Indians already living in the region. One group was the Santee. This tribe built huge earth mounds to honor dead chiefs and warriors. They placed the bodies on platforms over the mounds. Later, families removed the bodies, cleaned and oiled the bones, and saved them in a box. Other native groups included the Cherokee, Catawba, and the Yamasee.

First Europeans

The first Europeans in present-day South Carolina tried to build lasting settlements. Each time, they failed. Unsafe weather, Indian attacks, disease, and lack of food forced the settlers to leave. In 1526, Lucas Vázquez de Ayllón and 500 other Spaniards tried to start a settlement at Waccamaw Neck near what is now Georgetown. They died from fever and starvation. French settlers led by Jean Ribault failed to start a town on Parris Island in 1562. Four years later, the Spanish returned. They tried to build a town on Parris Island, but they left after 1586.

English Settlers

In the early 1600s, England claimed all of North America. King Charles I divided the area among some of his richest supporters. He gave one piece of land to Sir Robert Heath. Part of that land included present-day South Carolina. But Heath made no efforts to settle on the land.

In 1663, King Charles II of England turned the land of South Carolina over to leaders called Lords Proprietors. The Proprietors sent settlers to start Charles Town in 1670, which became Charleston in 1783. The Proprietors told the settlers what to do.

In the 1680s, settlers set up large farms called plantations. They found that rice grew well in the swamps near river mouths.

From Charles Town, the settlers shipped rice to Great Britain and the West Indies. Rich farmers brought African slaves to help harvest the rice and other crops.

The new settlers upset the lives of the American Indians. Settlers took Indian land without asking. To get their land back, the Yamasee fought with English settlers. During the Yamasee War (1715–1716), hundreds of settlers died

Settlers arrived in South Carolina by ship. They met many American Indians living near the coast.

Blackbeard

In South Carolina in the 1700s, the *Queen Anne's Revenge* was a feared pirate ship. This ship's captain was Edward Teach. His friends and enemies called him Blackbeard. Blackbeard had long, curly, black hair. Some people say he stuck slow-burning matches into his beard. Smoke swirled around his face, making him look scary.

Blackbeard died in 1718 in a bloody battle. According to stories, Blackbeard fought hard even after being shot and stabbed. After he died, the men who killed him cut off his head and displayed it on their ship. They wanted to discourage other people from becoming pirates.

in battles. Still, the Indians were not able to stop the settlers. Settlers forced the Yamasee out of South Carolina.

Colonial South Carolina

By the 1700s, Charles Town became a well-known port. Ships loaded with valuable goods sailed in and out of the harbor each day. Often, a pirate ship would overpower the merchants, board the ship, and steal the goods.

Colonists became upset with the way the Proprietors ran the colony. The colonists fought to change the leaders. In 1729, the Proprietors gave up their control. South Carolina was then ruled by a British royal governor.

The British government forced the colonists to pay taxes on tea, glass, paper, and other products. They taxed the colonists without giving them a voice in making laws.

The American Revolution

Colonists from South Carolina and the other 12 colonies led the start of the American Revolutionary War. The colonists wanted independence from Great Britain. In March 1776, South Carolinians forced the British governor out of Charles Town.

More Revolutionary War battles were fought in South Carolina than in any other colony. In June 1776, the British attacked Charles Town at Sullivan's Island. The colonists held off the British attack and kept control of Charles Town. The British failed to take over this southern port.

In time, the British won some key battles. In 1780, British General Charles Cornwallis took control of Charles Town. A few months later, British Lieutenant Colonel Banastre Tarleton killed 400 American troops at the Battle of Waxhaws Creek. He earned the nickname "Bloody Ban." The British also won the Battle of Camden in August 1780 to gain control of the entire colony of South Carolina.

U.S. troops won the Battle of Cowpens in January 1781 during the Revolutionary War. After pretending to retreat, the soldiers suddenly attacked. The attack surprised and overwhelmed the British fighters.

"I . . . am determined . . . to do everything in my power to see this once happy country enjoy its former liberty."
—Francis "Swamp Fox" Marion, American general during the Revolutionary War, in a letter dated September 24, 1782

Finding Ways to Win

The colonists had to think of new ways to fight the British. In the Battle of Kings Mountain on October 7, 1780, colonists hid among trees to surprise the British. Francis "Swamp Fox" Marion became famous for hiding in swamps and sneaking up on the British. At the Battle of Cowpens in January 1781, U.S. troops faked a retreat. When the British put down their guns, U.S. troops attacked. British troops had no training to defend these battle plans.

By 1783, American colonists had won the Revolutionary War. In 1788, South Carolina became the eighth state to approve the U.S. Constitution.

A New State

Over time, farmers in South Carolina began growing large amounts of cotton. After the invention of the cotton gin in 1793, farmers planted cotton all over the state. Many farmers owned small areas of land. They did not earn much money.

"Without a strong constitution to counteract the strong tendency of government to disorder and abuse there can be little progress or improvement."

—John C. Calhoun, Southern politician, born near Abbeville, South Carolina

Other farmers built plantations. Plantation owners became rich by trading cotton.

Growing and harvesting cotton took many workers. Many plantation owners bought slaves from slave traders. Most slaves worked long hours and had no rights. Laws stated that slaves were property. Children born to slaves would also be slaves.

After 1812, plantation owners started losing money. Cotton prices dropped. Plantation owners had a hard time growing enough cotton to make a profit. Growing the same crop on the same land year after year hurt the soil. Less cotton was being grown on the same amount of land.

Nullification

To make matters worse, the U.S. Congress passed new tax laws. Whenever another country brought items to trade in the United States, it had to pay a heavy tax. Countries stopped trading for U.S. goods. But South Carolina's farmers depended on selling cotton and rice to other countries. The farmers began to lose even more money.

In the 1820s, John C. Calhoun of South Carolina wanted to increase the state's rights. He believed the state had the right to declare unfair laws invalid, or null and void. With this theory of nullification, South Carolina claimed it did not have to follow certain laws. The state refused to charge taxes on imported goods. The state convinced the U.S. Congress to change the tax laws.

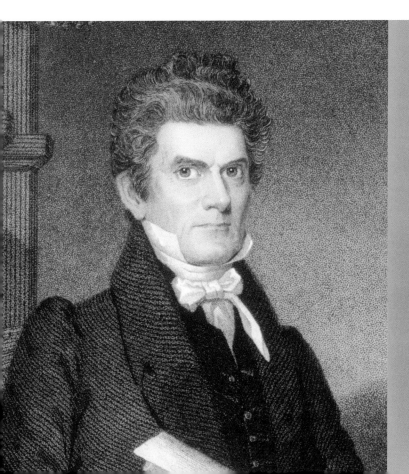

John C. Calhoun believed states had the right to refuse unfair laws.

Headed for War

In addition to arguing about states' rights, the U.S. Congress argued about slavery. Many people, especially Republicans from Northern states, wanted to end slavery. But Southern states did not agree. Without free labor from slaves, plantation owners would have to pay workers. Plantations would lose even more money. South Carolina threatened to leave the Union if a Republican won the presidential election.

South Carolina kept its promise. In 1860, U.S. voters elected as president Abraham Lincoln, a Republican who was against slavery. On December 20, 1860, South Carolina became the first state to leave the Union. Other Southern states followed. This group of states formed the Confederate States of America. The Confederacy readied for war.

Civil War

On April 12, 1861, troops from South Carolina fired the first shots of the Civil War (1861–1865). A battle for Fort Sumter in Charleston Harbor began. After 34 hours, the Confederacy controlled Fort Sumter. They kept control of the harbor for most of the war.

Confederate soldiers shot cannons across Charleston Harbor to attack Fort Sumter during the first battle of the Civil War.

The Union tried to make the South give up. Union General William T. Sherman marched his troops through South Carolina. He burned plantations and most of Columbia. By the time the war ended in early 1865, many men, women, and children had died. Almost one-fifth of the white male population of South Carolina had died in battle.

"If we accept . . . the face of discrimination, we accept the responsibility ourselves. We should, therefore, protest openly everything . . . that smacks of discrimination . . ."

—Mary McLeod Bethune, educator,
born in Mayesville, South Carolina

Rebuilding

The people of South Carolina needed to rebuild their state after the war. They set up a new state government. Laws had to be changed before South Carolina could become part of the United States again. South Carolina officially ended slavery. Men of all races could now vote. On June 25, 1868, South Carolina rejoined the United States of America.

The Civil War destroyed South Carolina's plantation system. Slaves were now free. Many African Americans moved north to find work. Others became farmers and worked the land.

Even though they were free, African Americans were still treated poorly. Jobs were hard to find. When African Americans found work, they were paid much less than whites doing the same work.

By the 1890s, the textile industry began to turn the state's economy around. Textile mills turned cotton into cloth. During World War I (1914–1918), mills in South Carolina supplied the armed forces with large amounts of cloth.

The Great Depression

After World War I, cotton farmers in South Carolina were still poor. Insects called boll weevils made matters worse. The insects ate through a part of the cotton plant called a boll. Without the boll, cotton could not grow. The insects destroyed the cotton crops in South Carolina.

During the Great Depression (1929–1939), people across the country lost jobs. They could not buy goods. In 1933, President Franklin Roosevelt started a job program called the

The Civilian Conservation Corps (CCC) planted trees in South Carolina during the Great Depression. The CCC program offered jobs to unemployed workers. They earned money while improving the nation's natural resources.

Civilian Conservation Corps (CCC). In South Carolina, the CCC planted trees and improved park trails.

World War II

World War II (1939–1945) helped South Carolina out of the Great Depression. The United States built military bases in the state. Military jobs strengthened the state's economy.

Because they lived on the coast, South Carolinians were fearful of German attacks. They watched carefully for submarines. They also tried to make their cities look dark by

Hurricane Hugo's strong winds and huge waves lifted boats out of the water, leaving them stranded on dry land.

turning off street lights and hanging dark curtains in windows.

Civil Rights

In the early 1900s, African Americans still did not have equal chances for success. Laws kept African Americans and whites separate. They went to different schools. At restaurants, African Americans could not eat in the same room as whites.

The Civil Rights movement that began in the 1950s changed the lives of African Americans. They became more involved in politics and the economy. In the 1960s, African American and white students began attending state public schools together. In 1983, South Carolinians elected African American civil rights leader I. DeQuincy Newman as a state senator. He became the first African American elected to the state legislature since 1888.

Hurricane Hugo

In September 1989, Hurricane Hugo blasted through Charleston and other coastal areas. Winds at the coast reached 130 miles (209 kilometers) per hour. Water rose as high as 20 feet (6 meters). Waves and winds knocked over bridges. Thirteen people died.

U.S. Senator Strom Thurmond greeted the press after he spoke nonstop for more than 24 hours in an attempt to delay a 1957 civil rights vote.

Chapter 4

Government and Politics

On December 5, 2002, U.S. Senator Strom Thurmond from South Carolina turned 100 years old. To celebrate, his coworkers and friends ordered a cake with red, white, and blue frosting.

Thurmond had a long career in the U.S. Senate. In 1954, Thurmond became the first person elected to the U.S. Senate as a write-in candidate. As he prepared to retire 48 years later, he was the oldest person ever to serve in the U.S. Senate.

During his long career, Thurmond proved he was able to accept change. At first, he strongly opposed civil rights measures. In 1957, Thurmond spoke on the Senate floor nonstop for 24 hours and 18 minutes to delay a civil rights vote. But in later

years, he changed some of his views. He hired African American staff workers and named African Americans to important positions. Many African Americans began to support him.

Branches of Government

The governor is the head of South Carolina's executive branch. The governor serves a four-year term and may be reelected only once. Other elected members of the executive branch also serve four-year terms.

The legislative branch of South Carolina is the General Assembly. Voters elect senators to four-year terms. Members of the South Carolina House of Representatives serve two-year terms. The assembly meets yearly to make laws. They also decide how to spend South Carolina's tax money.

South Carolina's courts make up the judicial branch of the government. The South Carolina Supreme Court is the highest court in the state. The assembly elects the chief justice

South Carolina's State Government

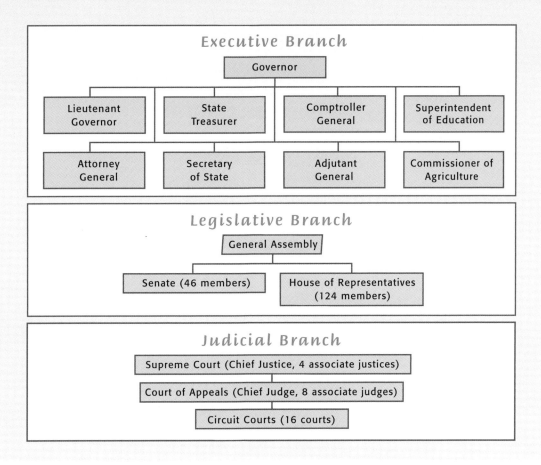

Executive Branch

Governor

- Lieutenant Governor
- State Treasurer
- Comptroller General
- Superintendent of Education

- Attorney General
- Secretary of State
- Adjutant General
- Commissioner of Agriculture

Legislative Branch

General Assembly

- Senate (46 members)
- House of Representatives (124 members)

Judicial Branch

- Supreme Court (Chief Justice, 4 associate justices)
- Court of Appeals (Chief Judge, 8 associate judges)
- Circuit Courts (16 courts)

and four associates for 10-year terms. A chief judge and eight associates make up the South Carolina Court of Appeals. They hear appeals from circuit courts. Circuit courts divide the state into 16 judicial districts. State legislators choose the circuit court judges for six-year terms.

The South Carolina state capitol in Columbia took 56 years to build.

Local Government

For many years, South Carolina's General Assembly members governed each of the state's 46 counties. Local state lawmakers controlled county finances. County commissioners did the day-to-day work. A home rule bill passed in 1976 gave more power to county commissioners.

Most South Carolina cities have a mayor and city council. In addition, large cities have paid city managers. Besides county and municipal governments, South Carolina has more than 600 multicounty districts.

Political Parties

Since the mid-1900s, South Carolina has leaned toward the Republican political party. In 1974, James B. Edwards became the first Republican governor of the state in 100 years. Since 1964, South Carolinians voted for Republican presidents in every election except 1976.

At the BMW plant in Spartanburg, workers inspect new cars. Manufacturing companies like this one strengthen South Carolina's economy.

Chapter 5

Economy and Resources

For years, South Carolina's economy relied on agriculture. Plantations leaned heavily on the use of slaves to earn money. When slavery ended, plantation owners no longer had free labor. South Carolina's economy changed to manufacturing textiles after the Civil War. Today's economy is balanced. Manufacturing, agriculture, and service industries make up most of South Carolina's economy.

Manufacturing

South Carolina is a leading manufacturing state. Top manufactured goods include aircraft, spacecraft, vehicles, paper, and plastics. Other companies make medical

"We cannot control the national economy, but we can fight to protect our jobs. Our nation must recognize the importance of a strong manufacturing base to our American way of life."
—Jim Hodges, governor of South Carolina from 1999 to 2003

instruments, electrical machinery, and knitted clothing. In 2001, manufacturing businesses sold nearly $10 billion worth of products to 183 different countries.

South Carolina has more than 371,000 manufacturing jobs. CropTech uses specially prepared tobacco plants to make medicines for cancer and other diseases. Some foreign-owned companies operate in the state. The German car maker BMW has had assembly plants in South Carolina since 1992. BMW recently spent $400 million and added 400 jobs to its Spartanburg plant.

Agriculture

Lumber is the leading cash crop in the Palmetto State. Most lumber comes from pines. Oak, gum, maple, ash, and poplar trees also provide lumber. Large commercial forests bring more than $650 million to the state each year.

South Carolina farm products are also important to its economy. Tobacco brings in nearly 25 percent of all

Trees grow close together in commercial forests. Lumber from the trees brings in most of the state's agricultural income.

agricultural income. Tobacco is grown mainly near the Great Pee Dee River. Farmers also grow cotton, soybeans, corn, and wheat. South Carolina is one of the country's largest producers of fresh peaches. It is second only to California in total peach production.

Fishing Industry

Along South Carolina's coast, many people make their living by fishing and catching seafood. Shrimp catches bring in the most money. Oysters, clams, and crabs also are caught. South Carolina makes $30 million each year from the fishing industry.

Tourism

Visitors spend $7.1 billion in South Carolina each year. More than 120,000 South Carolinians are directly employed by the tourism industry.

Many of South Carolina's 28 million yearly visitors head to outdoor areas. Sunny beaches are popular places. The northern part of the coastline is an almost unbroken beach. South Carolinians call it the Grand Strand. Myrtle Beach hosts the Sun Fun Festival every June. Nature lovers camp and hike in the mountains or at Congaree Swamp National Monument.

Many people travel to South Carolina to golf. South Carolina has more than 360 private and public golf courses. In South Carolina, people can golf every day for a year and never play the same course twice.

Colorful sailboats often line the shore at Myrtle Beach on sunny days.

The Gullah people of South Carolina's sea islands still honor their African roots.

Chapter 6

People and Culture

For many years, the Gullah people lived on South Carolina's sea islands without much contact with other people. The former slaves spoke their own language, a mixture of African languages and English.

Today, bridges connect most of the sea islands to South Carolina's mainland. But many parts of Gullah life remain unchanged. Mothers teach their daughters how to make sweetgrass baskets. Children learn Gullah songs and stories.

Some Gullah people still speak their own language. It is spoken softly, with rhythms that echo the Gullah's African roots. Some Gullah words have become part of the English language. They include "goober," "gumbo," and "voodoo."

Chitlin' Strut

For one weekend every year, Salley, South Carolina, becomes one of the largest cities in the state. The city's population swells from about 500 people to about 50,000 people. Since 1966, the town has held an annual festival called the Chitlin' Strut. Crowds of people, some dressed in hog costumes, line up for a taste of chitlins.

Chitlins, or chitterlings, are boiled hog intestines. Before cooking, the intestines must be carefully cleaned of fat and grit. Cooks cover the intestines with flour and seasonings. Finally, they boil the chitlins in hot peanut oil with vinegar, salt, pepper, and onions.

A Rich Mixture

When Europeans first arrived in South Carolina, most were from England. Later, German, Swiss, Austrian, Scots-Irish, and French immigrants came.

From 1850 to 1950, few people moved to South Carolina from other countries. After World War II, large numbers of

South Carolina's Ethnic Backgrounds

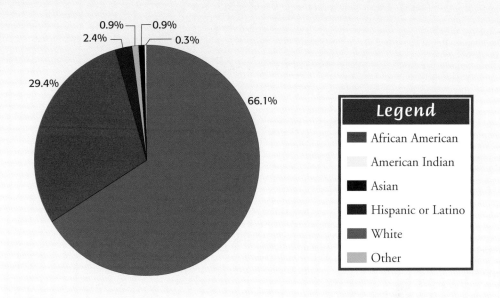

0.9% — 0.9%
2.4% — 0.3%
29.4%
66.1%

Legend
- African American
- American Indian
- Asian
- Hispanic or Latino
- White
- Other

Greeks and Lebanese came to South Carolina. East Indians, Vietnamese, and Hispanics moved to South Carolina's large cities in the 1970s and 1980s.

Many American Indian groups remain in South Carolina. About 2,500 Pee Dee Indians live in northeastern South Carolina. This number makes the Pee Dee the largest organized group of American Indians in the state. About 1,400 Catawba live on a small reservation along the Catawba River.

Sports in South Carolina

South Carolina has no major league pro sports teams. Instead, sports fans follow college teams like the Clemson Tigers and the University of South Carolina Gamecocks. Fans can watch football, basketball, soccer, and hockey.

Horse races are popular in South Carolina. The Carolina Cup race brings thousands of racing fans to Camden each year. Many families have reunions at this famous event.

From the Sea to the Mountains

South Carolina is a small state with a large past. Through the years, it has felt the damage of war and hurricanes. South Carolinians battled for America's independence and fought for states' rights. They learned from the errors of slavery and accepted equality.

The state's past made it stronger for the future. It faced the ghosts of its past and rebuilt. South Carolinians have grown strong in the face of change. Today, they celebrate and honor their roots.

Riders race their horses around the track at the Aiken Steeplechase, a nationally recognized competition.

Recipe: Gullah Rice Pudding

In 1685, John Thurber brought rice seeds to South Carolina. Rice soon became the state's main cash crop. During the colonial period, coastal South Carolina was the largest producer of rice in America. This traditional Gullah recipe uses rice to make a sweet pudding.

Ingredients

4 eggs
2 cups (480 mL) milk
1 tablespoon (15 mL) butter
½ cup (120 mL) sugar
½ teaspoon (2.5 mL) ground cinnamon
½ teaspoon (2.5 mL) ground nutmeg
¾ cup (175 mL) cooked rice
¼ cup (60 mL) golden raisins

Equipment

nonstick cooking spray
9-inch (23-centimeter) square baking dish
small mixing bowl
fork
saucepan
liquid measuring cups
measuring spoons
dry-ingredient measuring cups
wooden spoon

What You Do

1. Preheat oven to 350°F (180°C).

2. Spray nonstick cooking spray on baking dish. Set dish aside.

3. In a small mixing bowl, use a fork to beat the eggs.

4. In a saucepan, bring the milk to a low boil. Add the butter and the sugar. Stir constantly.

5. Add cinnamon and nutmeg to the milk mixture.

6. Pour the mixture into the baking dish. Add the eggs, rice, and raisins. Mix together with a wooden spoon.

7. Bake about 45 minutes until the top is firm and golden brown.

Makes 6 servings

South Carolina's Flag and Seal

South Carolina's Flag

On South Carolina's flag, a white crescent moon and palmetto tree are on a dark blue background. The palmetto tree honors the June 28, 1776, victory on Sullivan's Island. The fort there was made of palmetto logs. The blue background and the crescent are from the flag that flew at Fort Moultrie in 1776.

South Carolina's State Seal

On the left side of the seal, a palmetto tree grows from a fallen oak tree. It stands for the British ships that South Carolina defeated at Sullivan's Island in 1776. The Latin phrase "Animis Opibusque Parati" means "Prepared in mind and resources." On the right, the woman stands for hope winning over danger. The laurel branch in her hand stands for the victory at Sullivan's Island. "Dum Spiro Spero" is a Latin phrase that means "While I breathe, I hope."

Almanac

General Facts

Nickname:
Palmetto State

Population: 4,012,012
(U.S. Census, 2000)

Population rank: 26th

Capital: Columbia

Largest cities: Columbia,
Charleston, Greenville,
North Charleston,
Rock Hill

Geography

Area: 32,007 square miles
(82,898 square kilometers)

Size rank: 40th

Highest point: Sassafras
Mountain, 3,560 feet (1,085
meters) above sea level

Lowest point: Along the
Atlantic coast, sea level

Agriculture

Agricultural products:
Tobacco, beef, eggs,
cotton, soybeans,
corn, vegetables,
peaches, lumber

Climate

Average winter
temperature:
46 degrees Fahrenheit
(8 degrees Celsius)

Average summer
temperature:
79 degrees Fahrenheit
(26 degrees Celsius)

Average annual
precipitation: 48 inches
(122 centimeters)

Peach

Palmetto palm tree

Symbols

Bird: Carolina wren

Dance: The shag

Drink: Milk

Flower: Yellow jessamine

Fruit: Peach

Economy

Natural resources: Granite, limestone

Types of industry: Chemicals, textiles, machinery, rubber and plastics, paper, fishing

Symbols

Gemstone: Amethyst

Music: The spiritual

Songs: "Carolina," by Henry Timrod and Anne Custis Burgess; "South Carolina on My Mind," by Hank Martin and Buzz Arledge

Tree: Palmetto palm tree

Government

First governor: John Rutledge, 1776–1778

Statehood: May 23, 1788 (8th state)

U.S. Representatives: 6

U.S. Senators: 2

U.S. electoral votes: 8

Counties: 46

Timeline

State History

1500s
The first explorers to South Carolina meet many American Indians already living in the area.

1670
Settlers begin the first permanent English settlement in South Carolina.

1860
South Carolina becomes the first state to leave the Union.

1861
Confederate troops fire the first shots of the Civil War on Fort Sumter.

1788
South Carolina becomes a state on May 23.

1865
Union General William T. Sherman marches his troops through South Carolina.

U.S. History

1620
Pilgrims establish a colony in the New World.

1787
The U.S. Constitution is signed.

1861–1865
The Union and the Confederacy fight the Civil War.

1775–1783
American colonists and the British fight the Revolutionary War.

1914–1918
World War I is fought; the United States enters the war in 1917.

1963
African American and white students begin attending public schools together.

2002
U.S. Senator Strom Thurmond from South Carolina celebrates his 100th birthday on December 5.

1930s
The Civilian Conservation Corps plants trees and improves parks in South Carolina.

1989
Hurricane Hugo hits South Carolina in September.

1929–1939
The United States experiences the Great Depression.

1964
U.S. Congress passes the Civil Rights Act, which makes discrimination illegal.

1939–1945
World War II is fought; the United States enters the war in 1941.

2001
On September 11, terrorists attack the World Trade Center and the Pentagon.

Words to Know

barrier island (BA-ree-ur EYE-luhnd)—a long, sandy island that is built up by the action of waves, currents, and winds; a barrier island protects the shore from the ocean.

chitterlings (CHIT-uhr-lingz)—a food made from hog intestines; chitterlings also are called chitlins.

colony (KOL-uh-nee)—a territory that has been settled by people from another country and is controlled by that country

Gullah (GUHL-uh)—a culture started by freed African slaves living on the sea islands of South Carolina and Georgia

invalid (in-VAL-id)—not acceptable or legal

monadnock (muh-NAD-nuhk)—a small mountain that stands alone

nullification (nuh-luh-fuh-KAY-shuhn)—the act of making a law invalid

palmetto (pal-MET-oh)—a kind of palm tree with leaves shaped like fans

plantation (plan-TAY-shuhn)—a large farm where crops such as coffee, tea, rubber, and cotton are grown

proprietor (proh-PREYE-uh-ter)—a person given ownership of a colony

textile (TEK-stile)—a fabric or cloth that has been woven or knitted

To Learn More

Currie, Stephen. *Life of a Slave on a Southern Plantation.* The Way People Live. San Diego: Lucent Books, 2000.

Geraty, Virginia Mixson. *Gulluh fuh Oonuh—Gullah for You: A Guide to the Gullah Language.* Orangeburg, S.C.: Sandlapper Publishing Company, 1997.

Stein, R. Conrad. *South Carolina.* America the Beautiful. New York: Children's Press, 1999.

Weintraub, Aileen. *Blackbeard: Eighteenth-Century Pirate of the Spanish Main and Carolina Coast.* The Library of Pirates. New York: PowerKids Press, 2002.

Internet Sites

Do you want to find out more about South Carolina?
Let FactHound, our fact-finding hound dog, do the research for you.

Here's how:
1) Visit *http://www.facthound.com*
2) Type in the **Book ID** number:
   073682197X
3) Click on **FETCH IT.**

**FactHound will fetch Internet sites picked by our editors
    just for you!**

Places to Write and Visit

Angel Oak
3688 Angel Oak Road
Johns Island, SC 29455

Cowpens National Battlefield
4001 Chesnee Highway
Gaffney, SC 29341

Fort Moultrie National Historic Site
1214 Middle Street
Sullivan's Island, SC 29482

South Carolina Archives & History Center
8301 Parklane Road
Columbia, SC 29223

South Carolina's Governor
Office of the Governor
P.O. Box 12267
Columbia, SC 29211

South Carolina State Parks Service
1205 Pendleton Street
Columbia, SC 29201

Water falls more than 50 feet (15 meters) over lush plant life at Oconee Station Falls in northwestern South Carolina.

Index